Near and Far

by Katherine Scraper

I need to know these words.

library

mall

park

school

3

I made a map.
I put many places on my map.
Some places are near my home.
Some places are far away.

5

My school is near my home.

I can walk to school.
My friends walk to school, too.

The store is near my home.

I can walk to the store.

The park is near my home.

I can walk to the park.
I play ball with my friends.
We play ball in the park.

The library is far from my home.

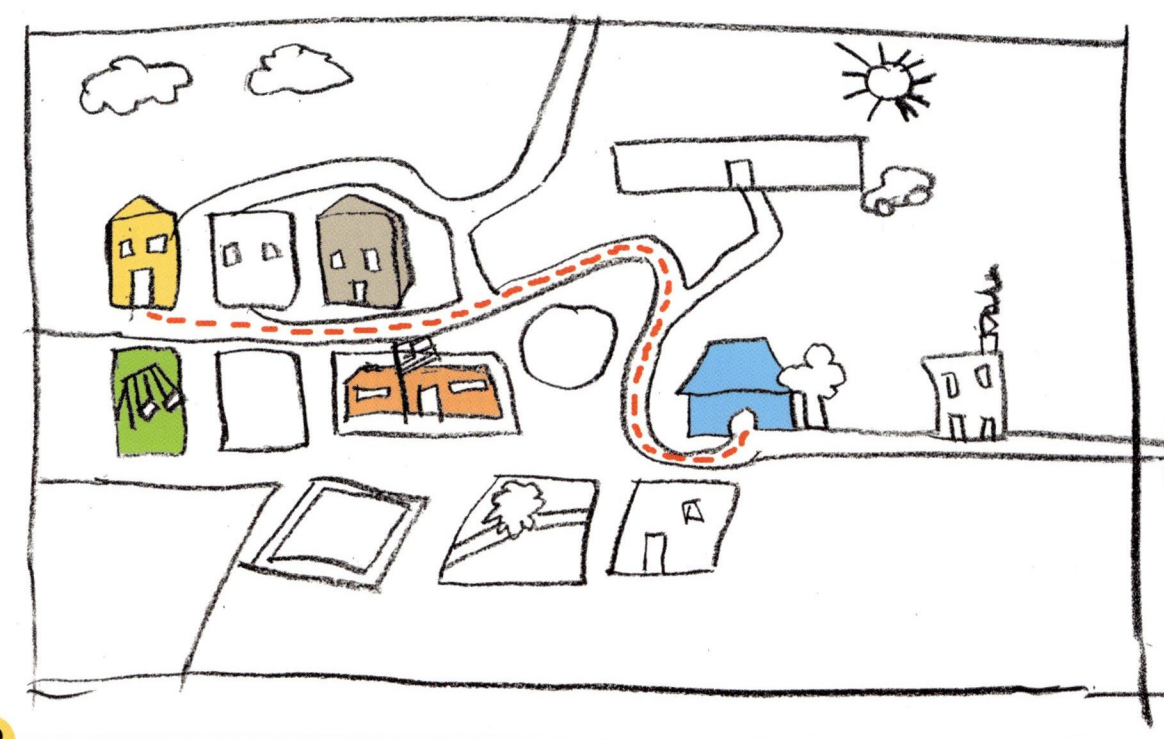

I can ride my bike to the library.

The mall is far from my home.

I can go to the mall.
My mom takes me to the mall.
I can ride in the car.

I can go to many places.
My map is the best!